How to Budget Like a Boss

How to Make a Budget and Stick to It, Get Out of Debt, Pay Bills and Save

Mike D. Moore

Text Copyright © Mike D. Moore

All rights reserved. No part of this guide may be reproduced in any form without permission in writing from the publisher except in the case of brief quotations embodied in critical articles or reviews.

Legal & Disclaimer

The information contained in this book and its contents is not designed to replace or take the place of any form of medical or professional advice; and is not meant to replace the need for independent medical, financial, legal or other professional advice or services, as may be required. The content and information in this book has been provided for educational and entertainment purposes only.

The content and information contained in this book has been compiled from sources deemed reliable, and it is accurate to the best of the Author's knowledge, information and belief. However, the Author cannot guarantee its accuracy and validity and cannot be held liable for any errors and/or omissions. Further, changes are periodically made to this book as and when needed. Where appropriate and/or necessary, you must consult a professional (including but not limited to your doctor, attorney, financial advisor or such other professional advisor) before using any of the suggested remedies, techniques, or information in this book.

Upon using the contents and information contained in this book, you agree to hold harmless the Author from and against any damages, costs, and expenses, including any legal fees potentially resulting from the application of any of the information provided by this book. This disclaimer applies to any loss, damages or injury caused by the use and application, whether directly or indirectly, of any advice or information presented, whether for breach of contract, tort, negligence, personal injury, criminal intent, or under any other cause of action.

You agree to accept all risks of using the information presented inside this book.

You agree that by continuing to read this book, where appropriate and/or necessary, you shall consult a professional (including but not limited to your doctor, attorney, or financial advisor or such other advisor as needed) before using any of the suggested remedies, techniques, or information in this book.

Contents

INTRODUCTION 5
CHAPTER ONE: PURPOSE AND GOALS 6
CHAPTER TWO: BUDGETING BENEFITS
.... 10
CHAPTER THREE: USING A HOUSEHOLD BUDGET
.... 17
CHAPTER FOUR: CHILDREN AND BUDGETING
.... 21
CHAPTER FIVE: MONEY SAVING IDEAS 30
CHAPTER SIX: EMERGENCY (SAFETY) SAVINGS CAN BE A FINANCIAL LIFE-SAVER ....
.... 34
ABOUT THE AUTHOR 38

INTRODUCTION

How to Budget Like a Boss.

I know what you're thinking. Just the thought of the word 'budget' is like nails on a chalkboard. I know the feeling.

For many years, I wouldn't have anything to do with a budget because I couldn't stand the idea of anyone—or anything—telling me how to spend my money. And where did that get me? Into a big financial mess.

Every month, when I ran out of money, I would turn to MasterCard and Visa for a bailout. Really bad idea.

What I learned from going through that experience and finding my way back to solvency is that, as much as we may loathe it, a budget is the ticket to financial happiness—not the straitjacket I feared it would be. I've come to prefer to call this a "spending plan" rather than a budget, but honestly the terms are interchangeable. It's just a way to pre-spend your income so that every dollar is assigned a job to do.

Like the blueprints to build your dream house, a spending plan shows you where you are and how to get where you want to be. It's the place where you spend your paycheck on paper even before you cash it.

A good spending plan gives every dollar a specific job to do. Once you have it just the way you want it, the plan becomes a handy road map for keeping your finances on track.

So, take a deep breath and let's walk through the basics of creating a simple budget that works for you and your family.

CHAPTER ONE

PURPOSE AND GOALS

This is your starting point. You must put your purpose and goals in writing. What is your purpose for saving money? What is your purpose for tracking your expenses? Why create a written budget? What do you want to accomplish?

Do you think about your purpose and goals? If you simply want to make ends meet each month, this is a goal. Everyone should have a purpose, which is linked to their goals.

A short-term financial goal is one year or less. You can have goals with shorter terms, but after one year, the goal becomes a mid-to-long-term goal.

Be passionate about your goals! Be sure to put your goals in writing. Don't be shy about telling others about your goals.

Goals will help you with money management. Without purpose and goals, many just spend money without a reason. Are you spending without a reason?

Goals should be a part of everything we do in our life. Goals can help you succeed with your needs, plus put you closer to your wants.

In many cases, the plan to achieve your goals is as important as the goal itself. Example: It's January and my goal is to save $10,000 for a down payment on a house, by December of this year. I will use a monthly written budget sheet to see where I can reduce my monthly expenses. I will put my money in high-interest savings or checking accounts, and each paycheck I will chart my savings goals. (There are banks paying higher APY in high-yielding checking accounts.) I will reduce, or eliminate dining out. I will reduce my vacation spending this year and find ways to earn extra money, such as a weekend, or evening job.

Making sacrifices, such as forgoing short-term pleasures for a year, is accepting responsibility to achieve goals. Be aggressive, passionate and driven about your goals. Map your steps with a written budget, then turn your goals into reality. Don't become discouraged if you have setbacks. So what if it takes an extra month or two to achieve your goals! Take pride in each accomplishment, and share your goals with others. They will be inspired by your successes. When you find goals you're passionate about, sacrifices become much easier.

It can't be stated enough to put your goals in writing. First, put three goals in writing, regard- less of the time frame. They can be short or long-term goals.

Basic Examples:

1. I will have 1.5 million dollars in cash when I plan to retire at age 65, and own my primary residence. I am 27 years from this goal, and my monthly budget (Spending Plan) is my map for planning and charting this goal achievement.

2. I will pay for my children's college education. This will take $100,000 and will need to be available in 15 years. I plan to use several college savings accounts to achieve this goal.

3. I plan to increase my income by $50,000 per- year during the next 24 months, by starting my own business in retail internet sales. My plan is to use my skills and talents I have acquired. This will require I put a business plan in writing.

Be very specific! - much more specific than these examples. Each one of these goals should take a page or more in details. Be very specific with dollar amounts, dates, and timeframe.

Be sure to examine and re-examine each goal. Your goals must provoke positive emotions. They must get you excited and give you a burning desire to achieve your goals.

For each long-term goal, you will need to have short-term goals of one year or less. These will be linked to your primary goal. This will help you achieve your main goal. For instance, in the retirement example, you would need to start an investment plan. Within your investment plan, you will have specific goals. Your budget will help you implement and achieve each of these goals.

Each goal will take on a life of its own. Don't let anyone tell you your goals are unrealistic! There are too many examples of people dreaming big and succeeding. Their reality became even bigger than their original goal - larger than they ever imagined.

Do not listen to people who say your goals are unrealistic… dream big and succeed.

The reason you must be passionate about your goals is simple: "Your drive and passion will keep your budget alive for the rest of your life."

CHAPTER TWO

BUDGETING BENEFITS

A budget is a document, or set of documents, used to record both actual and projected income and expenditures over a period of time.

The definition of a "budget" gives a good understanding of its purpose. We can draw from this description that a budget looks into our current and future financial picture. Not only can a budget predict our weekly, monthly, and annual expenses, but our income and savings as well.

A budget is our financial roadmap. We can chart our financial future with a simple written budget sheet. A budget can become a personal habit so we can control every dollar we accumulate. We can also create a plan to save for our financial and personal goals.

A budget does only what we tell it to do. A budget can reduce financial stress, by giving you a clear financial picture, and more control over your finances.

A budget should be a household habit that involves the entire family. Many studies have shown that most people learn about budging at home.

The benefits of a budget are easy to list, so take note and prepare to get started.

- By using a household budget, financial stress can be reduced by providing a financial plan.

- Budgeting promotes family values through financial decisions that relate to a family's goals and what is important to each of you.

- Budgeting is your map and plan to save money, by showing you areas you can reduce spending and increase savings to achieve your goals.

- Budgeting can help a miser find financial balance and a spender save. Remember, financial balance is healthy and an important goal.

- Budgeting will help you build a "Revolving Savings" and "Safety Savings" account in case of an emergency, such as a job loss, divorce, or a medical setback.

- Budgeting is your plan to a vacation, new home, or retirement. Also, it will provide motivation to improve your income through savings and goals achievement.

The starting point is to simply get started! You must know what to expect from your budget and why you are going to budget.

You must be willing to make changes in your life when dealing with your finances. If you continue to do the same things and expect different results, well, that is insanity. Be prepared to modify your harmful and wasteful habits for useful new ones.

Things to consider changing:

• You don't need a new vehicle every three years. Buy used vehicles and save thousands of dollars.

• Reduce spending on food and eating at restaurants… lattes and entertainment must be budgeted.

• "Brown Bag" lunches and take your lunch to work.

• Spend less on gifts for your friends - they will like you just the same.

You will begin to see many areas where you can reduce spending and change your financial situation.

Understanding the difference between Needs and Wants.

Example: A "need" is something that is necessary to keep the family and household working properly, such as new tires for the car, or a utility bill. Examples of a "want" would be a new big screen television, or new, brand-name golf clubs.

We need to identify some wants, as this is an area where many people struggle. We would like to think this is common sense, but it is not; people prove this each day by spending more than they earn, many times on unnecessary wants.

Examples of unnecessary wants that can break a household budget:

• Unplanned vacation with friends

• Anything customized on your vehicle

• Television cable beyond the basic

• Telephone caller ID, call waiting, camera phone

• iPod, Bluetooth, computer games, pool service, lawn service, over-gifting

• Latest electronic device to show off

Let's start by first looking at what you have done with your past finances. This will give you a starting point to build your future budget.

1. Gather your previous bank statements and checkbook records from the previous three months.

2. You will need all your sources of income. Gather documents such as paycheck stubs, SSI checks, child support received, dividend checks, etc.

3. If your income varies from week-to-week and month-to-month, average your income by totaling your monthly income for the past three months,.... then divide by three. This is a good number to start with.

4. We use a simple one-page budget sheet that emphasizes goals. For most of us, keeping our budgeting process simple is a recipe for success.

5. Start by filling in the income columns and enter the total. Use your Net Income. (This is your actual take home pay after taxes and other deductions have been taken out of your paycheck.)

6. Next is your Fixed Expenses. These are expenses that do not change from month-to- month, but are stable for at least six months. The budget sheet will categorize these items.

7. Flexible Expenses are items that you spend a different amount on each month. For most households, your largest Flexible Expense is groceries. Most people are surprised at how much they really spend on groceries each month.

8. Be sure to assign your money to a category and put all your money to work. If you find you have discretionary money (this is the money left after you subtract all expenses from your income), put this towards increasing your savings, then reducing debts.

9. If your budget is not in balance due to a shortage of money, then you will need to make adjustments; the easiest targets are Flexible Expenses to reduce your monthly expenses.

10. Using the goal side of your budget sheet, set a target goal to reduce your Flexible Expenses.

Example: Your actual (current) monthly grocery expense is $400. On the goal side of your budget sheet, set a monthly target goal of $370, then apply the $30 cost reduction to your credit card debt.

"Making sacrifices to achieve your goals takes maturity and discipline."

Using this process will reduce expenses within your monthly budget. If you are truly passionate about goals, you will find areas in your monthly budget to reduce expenses. Making sacrifices to achieve your goals will take maturity and discipline.

Be sure to customize your budget sheet for you and your household. Add items to your budget sheet that pertain to your unique monthly expenses.

Examples:

- Special food for your pet snake

- Special loans owed to family members

- Special work supplies

Let's look at monthly priorities that must be paid without fail.

Examples of Monthly Priorities:

Rent, mortgage, all necessary utilities, groceries, transportation, Insurance, and secured debt.

These items must be kept current and paid before other expenses such as unsecured debt (Credit Cards) are paid.

Use your gross income to determine if you are within the monthly general guidelines.

Example: Monthly gross income averages $3000, and your rent is $900. So $3000 X 30% = $900, and you are within the guidelines for monthly rent.

Areas to check to see if you may be overspending include: Transportation, Groceries, and Housing.

CHAPTER THREE

USING A HOUSEHOLD BUDGET

Be creative and make the budgeting process fun.

A simple tracking system for daily and weekly spending expenses is to use a 3"x 5" (or larger) spiral notebook. Write down how much you budgeted for the week, and stick to your budget plan.

Example:

Label a page for groceries. Your monthly grocery budget is $400. You go grocery shopping week-one and spend $75, so deduct $75 from your $400 on the grocery page. Now you have $325 remaining to spend on groceries this month. You can do this for most of your flexible expenses, such as:

- Groceries
- Gasoline
- Clothing

- Entertainment

- Spending money

- Gifts

This is an easy way to keep track of your expenses each week. Remember to plan for future expenses, such as... annual memberships, auto license tabs, and bi-annual auto insurance.

KEEPING YOUR BUDGET PROCESS SIMPLE.

Many financial counselors will have you complete a complex four-page budget (spending plan). This is not a simple process. For most of us, this can take the fun, and simplicity, out of budgeting.

These budgets will ask for gross income (before taxes and other deductions), then ask for all of your tax information and other deductions. To these counselors I ask, "What is the purpose of this exercise?" We are not looking for a Net Worth analysis but a simple spending plan. When we do a Net Worth analysis, we need more details and more financial forms for a complete financial picture.

Banks will not cash your Gross income. Only Net Income is usable for paying bills, Savings, and goal attainment.

Succeeding with your monthly budget takes consistency and discipline. Use your budget on a regular basis. Review it twice per-week, and make sure you're on track by looking at your financial accounts daily. A one-page budget sheet, as shown in this book, will help you succeed with your monthly spending plan and financial goals.

Most banks offer free online bill payment service. This is a much safer and less-costly method of bill payment and a very easy way to pay bills.

Advantages:

• No postage or envelopes to purchase

• Safety: No worry that your mail will be taken or lost from a mail drop box

• Convenience of paying bills anytime, day or night from anywhere

• Easy to set up automatic repeat bill payment

• A good method to track your expenses

- Review account balance daily if desired

Using on-line banking is a great way to track your monthly expenses. When reconciling your monthly budget, simply review your online checking statement. A very easy system to track all monthly expenses.

When reconciling your budget, you're checking to see if you stayed on track with your financial spending plan.

When you start a monthly budget, you are looking into your financial future. At the end of the month, you want to double check to see if your budget balanced, and you used good numbers. You do this by looking at your checkbook register, or online banking statement. Take each expense category, and total how much you spent for each budgeting category for the month. If you were tracking your expenses each week, you should be in balance.

Example:

In the Groceries category, you budgeted $400 for the month and tracked your spending each week. At the end of the month, you add all your grocery expenses and see you actually spent $420. Not bad, but you missed your goal. You will want to find where you spent the extra $20. Was it planned? Did you subtract $20 from another category, such as clothing expenses? If you did, then your budget balanced. You do this for each category to see if your budget balanced for the month. Moving money from one flexible expense category to another can help balance your monthly budget. This is being financially savvy.

CHAPTER FOUR
CHILDREN AND BUDGETING

Teaching your children the family's values about money is a family legacy.

A household budget should be shared with the family. Some parents may feel uncomfortable showing their children the household income.

There are ways around this. You can explain about expenses by going through the budget sheet and budget process with the family. You can exclude the income, and explain that it is private information.

Others will have no problem with this process, so showing income will not be an issue. Involving the entire family will increase the excitement and interest about saving and achieving the family's goals. Discuss financial issues with your children, and allow them to listen to the decision making process.

Example: Your family is planning and saving for a trip to Australia in two years, as a Long-term goal. (A short-term goal is one year or less.) By using a household budget, you involve each member of the family. Each can contribute savings towards this planned vacation. You can also give incentives for money-saving ideas.

Example: Your teenager decides to help by watching the younger children, allowing you to save money on a sitter and apply this savings to your vacation goal.

Teenagers involved in the budgeting process will learn to successfully manage their own money and set savings goals.

The payoff can be big. Children with money- management skills are less likely to have financial problems as young adults.

Parents need to take responsibility for their children's financial education, by teaching sound money habits. Eighty five percent of children learn about money from their parents. The teaching process can be easy. Take advantage of this, and be a good example. Remember to use leverage with allowance, and get their attention.

Allow your teenagers the responsibility of the household budget for a month. Let them make the purchasing decisions, and help them as they learn the process. Or have your teenagers plan their own financial spending goals by using a budget.

Since each situation is different, your challenge may be in getting your teenagers more involved with the budgeting process. Make an effort, because your family's financial legacy may depend on it.

Make sure you show your teenager the monthly bills. Show the cost of household amenities, such as the television cable, internet, and electricity bill, compared to an hour of work or their allowance.

When financial times are tight, and the household budget is challenging to balance, involve the entire family. Ask for ideas that can reduce monthly expenses. Review household luxuries that can be reduced or eliminated.

Today, many households are over-spending money on items that are not priorities.

Example:

Computer games, iPod downloads, or other monthly expenses associated with the internet. These are non-essential items.

Camera phones: Is it a phone or a camera? These are just a few examples of money pits that can upset a tight household budget.

Teaching your children to save and plan (wait for an item, instead of impulse buying) can be priceless. Items may go on sale at a later date, or a wanted item may fall out of favor with your child.

Giving an allowance to children is a great teaching tool. There are many parenting advantages to giving your children an allowance. Leverage is a big reason, and of course giving them the chance to manage their own finances is key.

Use the allowance leverage to your advantage. This is an added incentive for your children to follow the house rules and save money, by following their own budget. This should be the house rules of receiving an allowance.

Example:

An allowance for your five-year-old may be $3 per week. You can link chores to the money, so the child has the thrill of earning, saving, and spending money. One idea is to separate the money into five categories.

EXAMPLE FOR A FIVE YEAR OLD:

1. Spending money.

2. Short-term goals. (It's Important to start goal achievement early.)

3. Long-term goals, such as college or a bike.

4. Giving to charity or church

5. Holiday gift-giving.

This example is very general. Be specific with your children.

Make sure they are involved in each step of the budget and saving process. Keep them excited about their goals.

For children, a short-term goal would be 2—6 months. There are varying points of view on linking money to chores. There are chores each family member must do, and other chores can be linked to payment. Adults work for money, so there should be a connection between work and money.

Monthly Take Home Pay		
(Net Income) Take Home Pay		
Child Support / Alimony Received		
Other Income, Bonuses		
Total Net Income	$4,500.00	
FIXED EXPENSES	Constant for Six	

	Months
Mortgage / Rent	$1,300.00
Insurance: Auto, Home, Life	$140.00
Long Term Savings, IRA, 401(k)	
Emergency Savings	$300/Goal $15,000
Church Donations	
Legal / Child Support / Alimony	
Car Payment	$300.00
Total Fixed Expenses	**$2,040.00**
FLEXIBLE EXPENSES	**Change Month To Month**
Groceries: Household Items, Pet Food	$470.00
Cell Phone / Telephone	$150.00
Electricity	$150.00
Water/ Gas / Heat / Utility	$75.00
Bundle Package / Cable TV	$120.00

Internet Service	**Included**
Transportation: Gas, Oil Changes, Car Maintenance	$150.00
Credit Card Payment	$60.00
Other Unsecured Debt Payment Student loan, Bank loan	
Childcare / Daycare	$400.00
Prescriptions, Medical / Dental	$25 Copay
Pet Care, Postage, Office Supplies	$10.00
Clothing / Dry Cleaning	$40.00
Memberships / Contributions	
Home Maintenance	
Entertainment, Dinning Out Hobbies, Latte's, Movies	$300.00
Revolving Savings	$1000 Goal
Savings - College	

Spending Money: Hair, Smokes	$50.00	
Gifts / Holidays / Other		
Total Fixed Expenses	**$2,040.00**	
Total Flexible Expenses	**$2,000.00**	
TOTAL EXPENSES	**$4,040.00**	
Subtract Expenses from Income	*$460.00*	

Budget Goals	Budget Goals	
(Net Income) Take Home Pay		
Child Support / Alimony		
Other Income, Bonuses		
Total Income		
FIXED EXPENSES	**Constant for Six Months**	**Monthly Savings**
Mortgage / Rent		
Insurance: Auto, Home, Life		

Long Term Savings, IRA, 401(k)		
Emergency Savings		
Church Donations		
Child Support / Alimony		
Car Payment		
Total Fixed Expenses		
FLEXIBLE EXPENSES	**Reduce Flexible Expenses**	
Groceries: Household Items, Pet	**$420**	**$50**
Cell Phone / Telephone		
Electricity		
Gas / Heat / Utility		
Bundle Package / Cable TV		
Internet Service		
Transportation: Gas, Oil		

Changes, Car Maintenance		
Credit Card Payment		
Other Unsecured Debt Payment Student loan, Bank loan		
Childcare / Daycare		
Medical / Dental		
Pet, Postage, Office Supplies		
Clothing / Dry Cleaning		
Memberships / Contributions		
Home Maintenance		
Entertainment, Dinning Out Latte's, Hobbies, Movies	$250	$50

Revolving Savings		
Savings - College		
Spending Money: Hair, Smokes		
Gifts / Holidays / Other		
Total Fixed Expenses		
Total Flexible Expenses		
TOTAL EXPENSES		
Subtract Expenses from Income	*Monthly Savings*	$100

CHAPTER FIVE

MONEY SAVING IDEAS

• Many financial institutions offer high-interest savings accounts. Many have zero fees, with no minimum balance requirements. Some pay 1%-5% Annual Percent Yield (APY) during good economic times. This can be a great account for Safety Savings money.

• Clipping coupons and buying store brands. When done properly, a household can save over $1,000 per year.

• Carrying unmanageable debt is very expensive. Use a Debt Snowball to reduce your debt and save thousands each year.

• Raise the deductible limits on your home and auto insurance. Make sure you have this money in your safety savings account. This can save you $50 to $100 each month on insurance premiums.

- Stay within your written budget for all budget expense categories. Look for ways to reduce spending in your flexible expense categories.

- W-4 tax form: Adjust your exemptions to improve your interest-earning savings accounts.

Don't count on winning the lottery. Even if you did hit the "big one" a written budget is a must.

Invest your lottery ticket money into a high-yield savings account. The money saved will be a nice account after a few years.

Take time to be organized, and establish a good recordkeeping system; this will save you time and help with your money management. Make sure to keep tax records and important documents in a safe place; consider a fireproof safe for these documents.

- Brown bag lunch can save $50 to $60 per month.

- Bring your coffee from home. Not buying take-out can save $20 to $30 per month, or more.

- Never pay full price for any product where there is a commissioned sales person. Always negotiate a better price.

- When purchasing a commuter car for work, buy a used vehicle, with a four or six-cylinder engine, to save on gasoline and insurance costs.

- A home purchase is huge. Make sure you maintain your FICO credit score above 750. You will save hundreds each month. A higher credit score means lower monthly house payments.

- Save big on auto insurance with a high credit score, clean driving record, and life insurance for a multi-line discount.

Using a monthly spending plan and implementing a consistent savings plan is a great way to improve your net worth. Of course this can only be accomplished if you reduce your debt load also.

Monthly Savings (1) $550

Monthly Net Income (After Taxes) (2) $4500

Divide monthly savings by net income to find your monthly Savings Ratio.

Example:

(1) $550 Divide (2) $4500 X 100 = Savings Ratio 12.2 %

12.2% Savings Ratio is acceptable. Your savings ratio is a general guideline. There will be years this percentage will increase or decrease, depending on your household economy. A House- hold economy will cycle, the same as the American economy. In years where your household income is up and debt is low, be sure to save and plan for years when the house- hold income is down. Your goal is to find financial balance.

Let's look at your savings accounts. Savings are a big part of achieving your personal and family's financial goals.

CHAPTER SIX

EMERGENCY (SAFETY) SAVINGS CAN BE A FINANCIAL LIFE-SAVER

In cases such as job loss, medical setback, etc. For many households, the general rule of having a "Safety" savings account of four-to-six months' gross income will apply. Gross income is your income before taxes and other deductions are taken from your pay.

There are exceptions to the four-to-six month rule. For instance, those who are self-employed, and those who have income based on special, or specific talents, will want to build a larger "Safety" savings account. Up to one-year of income for loss of job or medical emergencies is recommended.

This emergency savings account should be in a liquid (easy access) account. This account should earn higher interest than a passbook savings account.

There are many high interest savings accounts paying 1—4%, and, depending on the economy, you may do better. It usually takes several years to build an emergency savings account, but it is important to have one.

A Revolving Savings Account (Top Priority)

A revolving savings account is, for many, an unfamiliar term. Simply put.... a revolving savings account helps balance a household budget when monthly unexpected financial surprises arise. This savings account will be a passbook savings account; usually at the same bank or credit union linked to your checking account.

Example: You did the household budget for the upcoming month. Your budget is in balance, and your teenager just remembered to tell you, he needs supplies for an upcoming science fair project, costing about $200. If the cost had been

$50, you could have moved money from the entertainment or clothing budget categories. Instead, use your "Revolving Savings Account." Move the $200 to the checking account to cover the added expense. Your budget will stay in balance without taking on additional debt.

Keep 20% of your monthly gross income in your revolving savings account. Income $3,200 X .20 = $640. This is your first line of defense from using a credit card for unexpected expenses. Build a Revolving Savings account before you build an Emergency account.

BUILDING USING A BUDGET

A budget is a great opportunity to start building wealth. There are several steps you must complete before you can start building wealth.

- Build a revolving savings account of 20% of your monthly gross income.

- Have a debt-reduction plan, such as a debt snowball, to pay off debt.

- Change the way you think about your financial situation and financial goals. Maturity and discipline are required to build wealth. If you continue to accumulate unmanageable debt by spending beyond your means, true financial wealth will elude you until you make changes.

- Create a savings plan using a budget to accumulate an emergency savings in case of job loss or medical setback. This account needs to be large enough to last your family from four months, to a year. Each family is different.

A single parent with children would need a much larger safety savings.

Your household budget can be used to accomplish many financial goals. Accumulating wealth takes knowledge and patience. The best method is to put your money into several financial investment vehicles, not just one. This can ensure you will never lose all your finances in one investment setback.

Take the time to learn about economic cycles and investment cycles. Understanding these two, may help "you" build financial wealth.

Those selling a "magic investment system" are only product sales people, not true financial educators. If their magic system really worked, would they sell it to us? They would be too busy using their system to make millions.

Slowly and steadily, save and invest for the long-run.

Budget and save 15—20% of take home pay, dividing this into several savings and investment portfolios. Be consistent and persistent to achieve your financial goals.

Plan for your future, and set financial goals that will allow you to retire from work in comfort and safety. A household budget can be used to plan and save millions of dollars for your future.

As stated in the goals section, dream big... save big. Don't allow debt to detour you from reaching your financial goals. Retirement should be one of your long-term savings goals. Learn the power of compounding interest, dividends, and leverage. Set a goal of saving at least 10% of each paycheck. Once you see your savings grow, your goals become reality. You will get more excited and want to save 20% each payday. How do you save a million dollars? One paycheck at a time. Start today and don't look back, only forward.

ABOUT THE AUTHOR

Mike Moore is an investor, business owner, blogger, financial advisor and author. He has been transforming lives with his books and blog posts. One of his latest books, *How To Earn Money While Sleeping* improved a lot of lives and he is working towards publishing more books.

He loves writing. He lives with his wife, Catherine in New York.

www.ingramcontent.com/pod-product-compliance
Lightning Source LLC
Chambersburg PA
CBHW070139230526
45472CB00004B/1608